THE MILLION DOLLAR PODCAST

BY JON ROBERT QUINN

Introduction

So, you want to build a podcast and from what it looks like you want to make a million dollars while you're at it. Well, I will show you how this is done. Now what I am telling you here isn't just in theory, this is what I have already done and continue to do every single day. When I started my first radio talk show on Money 105.5 FM in Sacramento, California, I already had maybe fifteen years of experience recording and producing music, so I had a thorough understanding of the equipment and software needed to build a quality talk show. I also had maybe ten years of sales experience, another tool vital for the success of my radio talk show business.

Here I am saying radio instead of podcast. Why is this? Is this because I'm an old-timer having been around the block a few times? That definitely has something to do with it, but the reality is, both are the essentially same thing. If you asked me when I got into this business if I was building podcasts, I would have been offended and pissed off because "radio" people consider podcasts as toys and built by amateurs. Radio was traditionally for big leaguers who are professionals. The reality however is that podcasts are NOW the new norm and radio is becoming obsolete.

According to experts, 70% of Americans now favour podcasts over conventional radio. Why is this? Well, the answer is simple. For radio, you have to tune-in at the specific time that the show comes on or you'll miss the show. If your reception is spotty, then you'll miss the show. If your phone rings and you have to turn down the radio, you'll miss the show. And, it's very expensive to build and air radio talk shows, sometimes costing thousands of dollars per week. And something that you may or may not have thought about is that you have to meet station and FCC guidelines. Some stations will allow some things that other stations may not. For instance, the stations I'm on don't allow cannabis or alcohol related products. That takes away from a lot of revenue I could be making.

So, why are podcast the new norm? It's simple. You can access the shows anytime, anywhere, any way you want to. They are available how you want them, when you want them, where you want them and you can start, stop, rewind, and listen again whenever and however you want. How is that not awesome?

OK. Let's talk about how to make this happen.

Setting Your Goals

When you want to build a talk show, you have to decide what you want to talk about. It has to be something people WANT to listen to and it has to provide value. If you provide people with something they need, they will buy your product. Now you're probably thinking that you aren't selling anything, it's a podcast right? How do you expect to make a million dollars if you're not selling anything? You have to sell advertising on your shows. You have to sell guest spots. DO NOT just put your friends on the show. This is a business. You must treat it like a business. If your friends are really your friends, they will want your success as much as you and they WILL pay to come on your show. If they don't, they are freeloaders or just don't need what you have to offer but REAL friends will buy your product anyway. Regardless, you have to sell yourself and your product.

You absolutely need to set realistic expectations for yourself such as sales projections, how many ads you'll sell in a day, week or month and create your routine on scheduling, recording and editing your shows. My suggestion is to build your show structure into a spreadsheet which I will show you later in this book. You will have to organise yourself and literally just fill in the blanks. I will also show you in this book how to make sales calls and sell your ads using the format from my best-selling book, The Cold Call King. This model has made me millions of dollars over the years and is used in sales organisations across the globe.

Everything you need to build, grow and maintain a success radio podcast business is in this book. Read it. Use it. Apply it. And make it your own. Your success depends on you.

Shift in Mindset

To be successful in this business, you have to change the way you think. If you're working a 9 to 5 job, that mindset will NOT suit you well in not only THIS business but in ANY business. If you are working for a wage, you are trading time for money. You need to quit thinking about how much time you have and start creating value in your ideas and create a product people need and sell it for what it's worth. Remember supply and demand and as your supply decreases, increase your price accordingly. This will weed out bad or troubled clients and allow you to keep more quality clients. If you have no idea what I am talking about, you will find out as you start to apply all of this into your business.

What else do I mean by shifting your mindset? You will definitely need to change your work ethic. You need a schedule and you need to stick to it. You cannot become successful with this unless you create a system in your day. You will make sales calls at one time, then record and meet clients at another time and then edit shows at another time. You want to stay on a strict schedule and remember this is a business. This will also allow you to see a progression in your growth. You may find yourself busy making calls and then later sitting on your hands because you have no clients to record shows with. Well you have to make a decision when this happens. If you can afford to take the rest of the day off, then do it. But if you're struggling to pay your bills, get your ass back on the phone and start booking interviews. The best way to succeed is to fail. But quitting is for losers.

By simply applying yourself, you will find yourself more organised, meeting great people and actually providing value to people in your community. Remember, with your podcast you're a problem solver. You have to provide them with a solution to a problem. Use your podcast is a way to help others get their message out to the public and as you make more calls, more people will be aware of your product. As more people are aware, they will listen. As they listen, your "play" analytics will grow helping you become more valuable to advertisers. Are you ready?

What is Money?

Money is nothing more than an exchange of value for value. Money isn't actually anything other than something of value that you trade for something else of equal value. If you're cold and it's raining outside and a guy is walking by with two jackets, you'll probably buy that extra jacket. This is no different with your podcast. There are business professionals, politicians, activists, hobbyists and more all around you and you have a platform to showcase those people to reach an audience they didn't have before you. This is your role. You are here to help these people get their message out to the public.

So, what is money? You are money. Your podcast is your money. Your talent is your money. You have value. We all do! You will only get out of life what you ask for. If you ask for $100 and can only provide $100 worth of value, then you'll have a hard time reaching that million dollars. BUT if you provide $1000 worth of value, it will become so much easier.

Is money a bad thing? Is money the root of all evil? I really don't think so. Money doesn't do anything other than accentuate the person you really are. If you're an asshole and you get rich, you'll likely turn into a bigger asshole. If you're generous and want to help people, not only will it be a lot easier for you to get rich, you'll become a better person and more valuable to more people. Are you ready to start making that money?

Getting Started

Ok. Here's where the work starts. You need gear. You don't need a lot of gear. You just need quality gear. Part of the success of your podcast is to LOOK professional so just having a microphone plugged into your computer not only LOOKS lame, it limits what you are capable of. Here's my suggestion. Either rent a small office for a few hundred dollars per month or take a spare room in your home and build a professional studio.

Start with a nice sturdy desk with microphones on both sides of the desk. You want your guest sitting across from you so make sure each of you have matching microphones, either cardioid or condenser microphones. Make sure you have headphones to hear the mix of the interview. Having a quality mixing board with USB input from the board into your computer is vital in today's day and age and you want a recording software like Audacity recording these interviews.

We will talk about show structure later in the book but I would recommend practicing on friends and getting comfortable behind the microphone before charging a penny to anybody. I really want you comfortable on the mic before you do anything. If you're not sure about what you're looking for, then look up my podcasts under Jon Robert Quinn on Spotify, TuneIn, or Luminary and study them. I was inspired and took my voicing and phrasing from Ryan Seacrest who was taught by Dick Clark. Every personality needs to create their own "personality."

Now that we have gone over what equipment is needed, let's get it all plugged in. Set your desk up and place your mixing board in front of you. Get two table mounting microphone stands, mount to the table and install the microphones. Run your XLR cables from your microphone into the mixing board. If the microphones are condenser microphones, make sure your phantom power is turned on. This runs electricity through the mic enabling it to operate. This is not needed for the cardioid microphone. If you want a quality condenser microphone, anything from AKG is good. Shure and Sennheiser both make wonderful cardioid microphones. A nice pair of AKG headphones will get you a quality monitor. The monitor is your ability to hear the quality of a recording. Run your USB from your mixing board into the computer and start recording. If you're not sure HOW to use a mixing board, I would suggest watching video tutorials

online. Ready for what's next?

Building Shows

Now that you have your equipment dialled in, it's now time to start building shows. Don't over-do it. Build one show at a time and build them into a series of episodes. I build my shows into a series of ten episodes. I do this so it's easier to manage and create continuity between these episodes. You want familiarity in the shows for your listeners. Your audience should almost guess what's coming next in your broadcast.

When building a show, you want to create the structure of the show. Now I wrote this book to teach you how to make a million dollars with your podcast and since I have already done this, the information I am giving is literally HOW I did it. If you follow the model precisely, you're be sure to get the same results.

When you build your show as a program interviewing guests, structure is very important. It should look like this:

•Opening Sponsor (30-seconds)
•Segment 1 Sponsor (30-seconds)
•Segment 1: Guest 1 (10-minutes)
•Commercial Break 1a (30-seconds)
•Commercial Break 1b (30-seconds)
•Commercial Break 1c (30-seconds)
•Segment 2 Sponsor (30-seconds)
•Segment 2: Guest 2 (10-minutes)
•Commercial Break 2a (30-seconds)
•Commercial Break 2b (30-seconds)
•Commercial Break 2c (30-seconds)
•Segment 3 Sponsor (30-seconds)
•Segment 3: Guest 3 (10-minutes)
•Commercial Break 3a (30-seconds)
•Commercial Break 3b (30-seconds)

•Commercial Break 3c (30-seconds)

•Segment 4 Sponsor (30-seconds)

•Segment 4: Guest 4 (10-minutes)

•Closing Sponsor (30-seconds)

Now what you're seeing here is structure. You're seeing what I call inventory. Imagine building this into a 10-episode series with a new episode every week. That would be 52 episodes per year. That means you can build a total of five series per year. Now let's look at what all of this looks like in terms of production.

You'll never record a show in one sitting if you want to create a quality product. Just like a television show, movie or music, it's all recorded in sections. Why is this? For one, you get continuity. Continuity is important. When you're selling your commercials, you sell for the series. When you're selling guest spots, you sell for the episode and segment. Sponsors are just a fancy way of saying commercial. I typically voice the commercial for my clients so they all sound like sponsors anyway and when I add music behind the voice, it really creates a nice quality sounding advertisement.

If you scheduled your interviews every day at 11a for instance, after four days you have one episode of interviews complete. Commercials can be recorded after the guest leaves and what's nice is, once the ad is recorded, save the ad in your archives and just copy and paste the audio into the sequence of your episodes.

Why would you want to have opening and closing sponsors? For one, it's money. For two, it's just nice to have "Tonight's broadcast is brought to you by...". It sounds professional and you're providing value to your clients. Imagine building all of this and working with a dozen or more businesses. You immediately become a celebrity in your community.

For your ten-episode series, make sure that each opening sponsor, each commercial break and each closing sponsor are the same. The only thing changing is the interviews in the content. Well how do you catalog all of this content once it's complete? By the clients name of course and what's really cool is, these clients will take pride in their interviews and share this content on their social media and website, increasing your traffic and giving you the analytics you need to sell more and higher priced ads making you more valuable. Is it starting to make sense yet? Keep reading!

Finding Guests

Now I know you're probably thinking how in the world do you sell four new interviews per week. It's easier than you think! You have to create your website and create the buzz. Get on social media and create beautiful channel art or artwork for your show. You probably already work with some local businesses or know people who own business and start talking to them about your new show. If you have a quality model and it looks professional and you have a good reputation in the community, you'll have no trouble selling ads.

My first interviews I sold for $700 each. It was very challenging at that price yet that was for four segments or one full episode. Shortly after, I went to $499 for two segments which became easier for small business owners to afford and by using simple math, made me more money. Today, I sell interview for $199 and sell four per show, plus sell the commercials and sponsor inventory too. This makes for a very lucrative living. Today, I have 21 talk shows and have no intention to stop making shows. Think about the revenue I am creating by helping businesses reach a new audience. The funny thing is, today my phone rings for people who want me to showcase their business because clients tell their friends and refer business to me.

So how to you find guests? The following few chapters will be taken literally from my book The Cold Call King. This is a sales method I have used to sell inventory in shows but basically shows the steps to cataloging local businesses and how to reach out effectively and efficiently, ensuring you close more deals. Here's a little sales training.

When you're building your business, the most important form of marketing is word of mouth. Do you agree? If not, then you really need to listen up. Your friends, family and past clients will literally make or break your business. If you are not getting repeat business and the community isn't talking about your product, then how do you plan on surviving?

Imagine if every single one of your clients gave you a referral every single time they did business with you. What would that do for your business? You would probably do pretty well. Don't you think? Not only do I think so, I know so. Now think about those referral clients now coming in to see you and now giving you their referrals. What would that do for your business then? It sounds pretty awesome doesn't it? That is what I am going to challenge you to do.

Regardless of the business you're in, whether it's car sales or dentistry, I want you to try this! Call five of your best clients and ask them for a stack of business cards of their clients or contacts. Make sure they know they will never see those business cards again. Most business professionals have about a hundred business cards in a drawer of people they frequently use or have run into along the way. A lot of business owners even have stacks of junk cards by people they have never done business with. Those are great too. In return you will give them about the same amount of business cards from your contact list. Now, I want you to catalogue all of those names, email addresses, and phone numbers in an Excel Spreadsheet. I will explain how I want this done later. In the meantime, keep reading.

Next, I want you to call the next top client of yours and do it again. I want you to do this consistently adding new people to your list every single week. You will find yourself with thousands of names, email addresses and phone numbers in your database in no time at all. Make sure of two things.

1) Make sure when you list the name in excel, you include who referred the client.

2) Make sure you're moving the cards along to your next client. Client one's cards now go to client two. Client two's cards now go to client three and so on.

Your Contacts

It is very important that you use your list exactly like I recommend. I have used this formula for over a decade and have made millions of dollars using only Microsoft Excel and my cell phone. When you start using the formula for yourself, you will see how easy and efficient it really is.

Step 1: Create a New Spreadsheet.

Step 2: Understand the Columns.

Column A: Client's Name

Column B: Type of Business

Column C: Phone Number

Column D: Email Address

Column E: 1st Attempt Contact (leave blank)

Column F: 2nd Attempt Contact (leave blank)

Column G: 3rd Attempt Contact (leave blank)

Column H: Name of source of Referral

Step 3: Understanding the Colour Chart

White: Lead not yet touched

Yellow: Attempted Contact, No Contact

Orange: Contact Made / Follow Up

Burgundy: Not Interested or MIA

Red: DNC or Do Not Contact

Blue: Sold Deal but Not Closed

Green: Closed and Paid

Step 4: Understanding Pages

You'll see Sheet 1, Sheet 2, Sheet 3 at the
bottom of your spreadsheet. I want you to change

those to A, B, C, D, E, etc. All the way to Z. On each of these pages, you will put the lead's first name accordingly on those pages. This allows for easy organisation and quick reference. You want to be able to click A and see every client with the first name starting with letter A. You will also be able to see how many Yellow, Orange and Blue deals are available and need to be contacted. You do NOT need to type in notes on any of these files. You should be able to determine the status of every lead quickly by understand what colour is being used.

When you're looking at a page of leads and you see Yellow, you'll know immediately that you have not spoken to this person and there may be a deal there. Call them and try moving the deal forward. When you see an Orange lead, you'll know that you have made contact with that person and there may be some interest there. Call them and try moving the deal forward. When you see a Blue lead, you'll know it's a sold deal but are waiting on payment. Call them and get an ETA for payment. Your goal is to get every deal either Red for DNC or Green for CLOSED.

The Cold Call King System

Now that you have input your leads into the spreadsheet, it's now time to understand HOW to execute the Cold Call Process. There are two ways to make cold calls. The right way, where you get results and people want to do business with you. Or, the wrong way when people hang up on you and block your number. I can honestly say that when I make my cold calls today, maybe one person per month will actually hang up on me and that is simply because I am non-intrusive, and I follow the system precisely to ensure that I get the results I expect. I am polite and not pushy but am always on high alert looking for an opportunity to close a deal.

Before you make ANY calls, you need to attempt contact another way first. That first initial contact should ALWAYS be by email. If you cannot find their email address, most often times if you take that person's name and phone number and punch them into Google and type email address, you will find it. The email you send should be a form email that goes to every single person consistently. I like to send an email maybe one a week to all of my thousands of contacts. Most often times, it will end up in a junk folder, but that is okay. The point is to make contact and have an "in" when you call them. Now, after you have sent that FIRST email, make sure you update Column E with today's date and mark it Yellow. Two things happened. You attempted contact with the email and Yellow means a contact attempt was made.

A lot of companies use Salesforce or other CRM systems to conduct daily business. They say it's efficient. There's one issue with these formats. Most companies want notes taken after each attempted call or after a phone conversation explaining what happened on that call. Here's the way I see it. WHO CARES WHAT HAPPENED? THEY DIDN'T BUY ANYTHING. So, why put notes at all? By simply marketing it Yellow tells you that you've attempted contact and got nowhere. That means to try again later.

I would recommend calling leads two to three days apart. Don't hound people but make yourself present. Don't be afraid to hop on Facebook and add them as a friend as well. They may already be friends with you and know all about what you do but are just too busy to answer or don't recognise your phone number. Regardless, unless they say never to call again, there's probably a deal there.

Making Calls

You're going to have to trust me on this and follow my directions precisely. I guarantee that you will get into your own head and let your ego dictate what happens here, but that is only going to make yourself inefficient, effecting how the system works and how many calls you make. You want results, right? Then do it exactly like this!

Now that it's time to start making calls, you need get your phone out and set it in front of you and preferably on speaker phone. You are going to make four calls per minute using this system. If they answer, keep the call to under one minute unless there are buying signs. We will get into those later. The point here is to reach as many people as possible in one sitting. I can make three hundred calls in an afternoon or as many as five hundred in about six hours of calling, closing several deals and talking to as many as twenty-five or more people.

Make sure that when you're making calls, your spreadsheet is right in front of you and ready and DO NOT GET BORED. Have excitement in your voice and make sure you follow my lead-in.

Step 1: Dial the number

Step 2: Put it on speaker phone

Step 3: Only let the phone ring for 15 seconds

Step 4: If no answer after 15 seconds, hang up

Step 5: Mark today's date in Column F

Step 6: Immediately dial the next

Two things will happen, either they answer, or they don't. DO NOT leave a voice message. Ever. Why? For one, you're burning valuable energy speaking when you don't need to be. Two, they will never call back a salesperson. Three, you're wasting time when you could be making more calls. Four, if they see a missed call, chances are they will call back giving you an opportunity to close them.

If they do answer, your conversation should remain under one minute UNLESS they are genuinely interested. Buying signs are important to identify. If they start asking questions about the product and start placing themselves in the situation, chances are they are interested. Don't be afraid to ask them about their current product and whether it's working out for them or not. This gives you an opportunity to find a solution to a problem and make the deal.

When they answer, use this "script". Please make it your own, but make sure you say it exactly the same way every single time. Here's the one I use.

"Hello Joe? (wait for them to respond). Hey, this is Quinn from The Good Life Show on 105.5. I just wanted to circle back around and see if you had a chance to review the information I sent regarding showcasing your business on our show."

Two things will happen, either they saw the information, or they didn't. We are referring to the email we sent them days prior.

If they saw it, ask them if it looks like something they would be interested in. Do not be pushy. These people do not know who you are. Most times, they will not have seen the email. Here is your follow up.

"Ok, here's what I will do. I am going to send you a quick text message with the information and a link to our website. Please take a moment to review it and see if it looks like it'll be a good fit. I will circle back around next week. Does that work for you?"

Two things will happen here. If they say, "Sure", it usually means they are taking even a little interest. Mark it Orange and follow up in a few days. If they say "No", it means they're not interested. Simply mark the file Burgundy and type Not Interested in Column F.

Now, if you made contact and they show a little interest, send them the text message as promised and mark the file Orange. Circle back around in a few days or week. Do not bombard these contacts however, stay on them. I have more people tell me it's impressive at how persistent I am and eventually do business with me, than tell me to never call again and hang up on me. If you're non-intrusive, you will get business from these people sooner or later.

Even if you mark a file Not Interested, you will still be contacting them again in a few months. I love seeing Not Interested leads turning into Closed deals. It happens all the time. Just be patient.

After you have:

1) Sent the email in Column E

2) Made the initial call in Column F

3) Attempted again in Column G

4) And still no answer by attempt 4…

I want you to mark the lead Burgundy and move on. When you get to the end of your list from A all the way through Z and everything is marked either, Red for DNC, Burgundy for Not Interested/No Contact or Green for Closed, mark ALL of the No Contact leads Yellow and work them again. There are deals there. You just have to find them. What you will find is that people that you have tried calling before that never answered their phone are now answering giving you an opportunity to make the deal happen. Maybe they have been getting all of your emails and haven't needed your product until now. Don't be afraid to text some of these people if you're not getting anywhere with them. If I get to the end of a lead with 4 attempts and never made contact, I will send a quick text with who we are and what we do with a link. There are times when I get an, "I'm Interested". Immediately, I pick up the phone and call them and now we have a deal.

Now, what does Blue and Green mean? Earlier, I said Blue was SOLD and Green is CLOSED. Aren't those the same thing? The answer is NO. How many times have you had a client interested and once you sent the invoice to be paid, they just disappear and never pay the invoice? It happens very very often, especially the business I'm in. So, BLUE means that they are interested, and we have sent out the invoice but are waiting for payment.

Here is a very important lesson for you. DO NOT CHASE PEOPLE DOWN. If they are going to pay you, they will. If they don't, move on. So, in order to handle this, when somebody becomes interested, mark the lead BLUE and in Column E, put today's day and let them know that payment needs paid in however many days you're willing to wait. I tell my clients seventy-two hours. I will make three attempts to follow up regarding collecting payment. A few days after I send the invoice to the client, I will reach back out again and put that date in Column F, then again, a few days later in Column G. And if no payment a couple of days after that, I mark it Not Interested, colour it Burgundy and move on to the next lead. A client that is a pain in the ass before getting paid will be an even bigger pain in the ass after getting paid. We're in the business to make money, not babysit adults.

What happens after payment comes in? Mark it GREEN and move onto the next client. Congrats, you've made money and after providing services, ask them for business cards to add to your list and keep moving the leads forward. Make sure to follow up with your clients periodically. Make sure you're providing them value and quality. Don't be afraid to ask them for reviews. By simply following up with them, this opens new conversation for future repeat business. Usually when you work with somebody more than once, the deals get bigger and bigger because trust is built, and you have followed through with quality and service.

Referrals

Earlier in this book I mentioned Column H containing the name of the person who had supplied the lead's name. Make sure you are giving back to your clients who are helping you succeed. This column is a very important tool and serves two purposes. I make sure to give my clients who refer business to me twenty percent back in credit to be used toward more of my company's services. If the person they referred spends a thousand dollars with me for instance, that client who referred them to me now has a two hundred dollars in credit for more services which comes in hand around renewal time.

The second reason for having their name in Column H is for when the prospect you're talking to asks where you heard about them. Having that name handy makes the whole conversation shift into friendly banter. Once that conversation shifts to a friendly one, you can now talk about your relationship with that person and get to know their relationship. After the call, they usually go back to the person who referred them and helps that client move toward doing business with your company. This is the proper use of word of mouth advertising. You have a community around you. Use it.

I think where people get work of mouth advertising wrong is when they WAIT for people to talk about your business. Unfortunately, you cannot wait for ANYTHING in business. YOU have to be moving forward and creating innovative ways to reach new people. Look around you. There are hundreds, if not thousands of like business in your community. Who are the people doing well and what are they doing different? If you continue to do the same thing as everybody else, how do you expect your business to stand out from the rest? If the majority of like businesses in your community are just getting by and you're doing the same marketing and have a comparable product, how could you expect your business to be any better than the competition? You can't, and you won't and if the market shifts in any way, the weaker businesses will be swept away by the stronger ones.

Rebuttals

With making sales calls every day, there is a one hundred percent change somebody will not want what you're trying to sell. There is nothing wrong with somebody telling you they aren't interested or that your price is too high. What is wrong however, is how you handle those rebuttals and how you bring that potential client closer to a sale.

There are pushy rebuttals that will kill your deal or any chance of a deal and then there are the rebuttals that answer the questions and remove doubt. What are they and how do they work? The last thing you want to do is piss somebody off who is just asking qualifying questions to see whether or not you can provide them with value. Believe me, I have pissed plenty of people off and killed more than enough deals.

The most common "excuse" I get is "I'm not interested". When I was selling cars, hanging up after a client said they weren't interested was a major no-no and sometimes an offence that would get you fired. Before we get into the meanings of "excuses", let's get into identifying what the excuses actually mean.

When dealing with the public every day, I see most people making a major mistake in HOW they listen to words people say. It's like that person that talks behind your back and spells out your every flaw. It's not they hate you, but rather they envy you and their insecurities are fuelling their trash talk. You'll never hear an ugly person say that another person is ugly. It's always the pretty person but the pretty person feels ugly inside and then saying the other person is ugly makes themselves feel better. Does that make sense? So instead of listening to their words of how ugly that person is, listen to the story of why that person is saying what they are saying.

Here's another example:

Mary had a little lamb. What does this mean? Does she have the lamb, or does she no longer have the lamb? If you listen to the words, it says she no longer has a lamb. However, if you listen to the story you'll know she still has the lamb. You need to apply this thinking into every single transaction you encounter. Apply this to your daily life as well too. You'll find yourself reading people better than the guy next to you and this always giving you the advantage.

When I check in to a hotel, I always ask for a discount, but I never actually ask for the discount. I use a story rather than words and that creates action. I walk in to the hotel and check-in and the host tells me the room is two hundred dollars per night plus twenty-five dollars per day for parking. I'll respond with, "Oh sheesh. I didn't know I was paying for parking tonight too. Sigh. Are there any programs or incentives I could apply for that would wave that by chance?" Often times, they will just wave the fee and with a smile and eye contact, thank them. I never actually "asked" for a discount, but I got it exactly what I wanted. Now, let's apply this to cold calls.

What does "not interested" actually mean? Either they are busy and want to get off the phone with you or they are really, just not interested. So, when they say they aren't interested, a simple rebuttal of, "let me ask you something, did you have a chance to see the information we sent over to you?" They will either respond with a yes or no. If they say yes, then respond with, "So you read about what we can provide you and you just don't see any value in what we can provide you?" This will open up the conversation. If you aren't getting anywhere with the transaction in a reasonable amount of time, mark the date on Column on E, F, or G and move on to the next lead. If they respond with no, they haven't seen your information, then send the text message and tell them you will follow up in a few days.

One of the things I have learned after two decades of sales is, these people are adults. You shouldn't have to strong arm anybody to buy your product. Keep them in your database and keep calling them according to this system. Eventually, they will buy from you or tell you to remove them from your list. This brings me to an important point. If somebody says anything like, "remove me from your list" or, "don't call me anymore", you are required by law to remove them and refrain from ever contacting that person again, UNLESS they opt back in for contact.

Here's the next excuse. I get this one all the time and there are a few ways to make this one work. "I can't afford it."

This is not as common for smaller purchases but very common with new car purchases. I get this one all the time selling advertising for small businesses. This is also very easy to overcome if, done properly. "I can't afford." "Let me ask you... What if I could not make it fit into your budget, but actually save you money each month?" Now you are piquing their interest and finding a solution to a problem. Again, you were non-intrusive and not pushy. When I hear this excuse when calling small businesses to sell advertising on my talk shows, I always ask, "What if I broke it up into payments over twelve months?"

Let's say a customer is looking at a year's worth of advertising and the total is two thousand, four hundred dollars. A lot of small businesses don't have that kind of money laying around, especially for advertising. They know that they need the product for their business but spending a lump sum like that hinders the reserves for that business. By offering the same product for two hundred dollars per month, we close the deal, improve their business and six months down the road when business has picked up, we can offer them more of our products. But, had we not found a solution, we would get nothing. Not a deal, nor the relationship and the referrals that business sends our way.

Sales is nothing more than providing a solution to a problem. All we need to do is find out WHAT that problem is, and we have earned the customer's business. Years ago, I created an acronym for SALES.

Simple And Less Expensive Solutions

A sale must be **easy** for the customer. A sale must provide the customer **value**. And, a sale must provide a **solution** to a problem.

Have you heard of the 3P's or 3M's in a Sale?

Person, Price, Product or Man, Money, Machine.

Both are the same thing and apply to every single transaction the same way. The customer must LIKE YOU, THE PRICE, and/or THE PRODUCT. If they don't like TWO of any of those things, you have NO DEAL.

However, the price could be right for the customer and product could be exactly what they are looking for, but if they don't like you, you have NO DEAL. So, when you're making your cold calls, if you're pushy and you cannot quickly identify their problem and provide a solution to that problem, chances are you won't get the deal.

Understanding Marketing

The formula for marketing is very simple when you dumb it down. If you follow this very simple formula for your small business, you'll do very well. It's when you start getting into analytics and trying to use a big business' formula that you start wasting time and making yourself less efficient, which in turn, costs you money.

Frequency and Reach

What does this mean? Marketing is nothing more than frequency and reach. How many people can you reach? How many times can you reach them and how many different ways can you consistently reach them?

If you slowly start adding the leads in your spreadsheet as friends on Facebook, Instagram and Twitter, they will start seeing your posts. They will see your friend's posts. They also see your friends of friend's posts. Then, when they see your emails and even your text messages, you're starting to now make a positive impression. And then when you call, these people are already becoming familiar with what you do and will either be interested or not interested what you provide. The community turns on the radio, there you are. They see your advertising on Google and other various websites. They see your posts on Facebook, Instagram and Twitter and start liking or even sharing your posts. Then what happens when you're speaking at an event or presenting before a group of people? Now you have credibility to go with it. Then one day, you're in public at a restaurant or supermarket and they walk up and introduce themselves and say hello, what is going to happen when they need you or your product or services? Who will they call? You. Why? Because you made yourself available to them and you stood out from your competition. If you keep doing the same thing as everybody else, how will set yourself apart?

Here's my next piece of advice. Whoever you are and what you've done, nobody cares. It sounds harsh but the reality of it is, all they care about is what you can do for them. If you cannot provide them with value, all of your awards and credentials don't mean anything. Make sure you can provide value, or you've got nothing.

Where do you start with your marketing? Large companies have millions and millions of dollars set aside just for marketing their business or product. This turns into future revenues to be budgeted for future marketing to create their business' cycle. With a small business, you don't have the millions of dollars sitting around to advertise your business, but in today's world, small businesses DO have the advantage. More people than ever want to work with small and locally owned businesses. They want to keep the money local and word of mouth advertising is what does this. You start with trading business cards like I mentioned before. Then work on your social media presence. Then look for local media forms like radio, tv, and magazines. Make sure to find cost effective mediums and don't be afraid to get creative. Get to know your local radio hosts. Talk to them about using your products and endorsing you in trade. The same goes for television personalities, magazine editors or even newspapers columnists. I hear people all the time say that the newspaper is dead. If that's the case, why is it still profitable? Because newspapers are online now and, on our devices, connected to social media. There is still a huge audience for print however, most news is delivered digitally today.

Repeating the System

It will take some considerable time to get through all of your leads, especially if you continue to grow your list. But, what happens when everything is marked, GREEN for Closed, Burgundy for No Contact or Not Interested, or RED for Do Not Call? The answer is simple. Mark all of the leads YELLOW, that you never got a hold of or the deal went nowhere. Start at letter A and start working the list again. You will now find that a lot of people know who you are may want to proceed.

Here's another issue you may run into. What happens if you're talking to a potential customer and they ask to follow up in six months? In Column E, type "Call July 6th" or whatever date you two agree on, mark it ORANGE and follow back up on that date. There is nothing wrong with keeping tabs on your potential deals. Please don't make the mistake of needing a ton of notes in your system. Notes mean nothing if they aren't buying anything.

What about if you're just not that good at sales? What if you're a beginner? What if you have never made cold calls before and you're afraid of rejection?" These are all questions I get all the time. If you're afraid of being hung up on, then get hung up on. Dust yourself off and do it again. It's no different that asking a pretty girl or cute guy out. If they say no, you'll probably try a different way another time and hope for a yes. Eventually, somebody else will come around and you'll get your shot. And then when that happens, you'll feel like stud and go for another one. It's not rocket science. You just need to be patient and persistent.

What happens after the deal is made? I personally like to follow up with my clients consistently and see how well I am doing. Sometimes, I get news I don't want to hear, and they tell me that I let them down. This is where I can try to make it up to them, provide more value and possibly even make another deal with the client which is great for business. Just make sure that you're true to yourself and you're providing quality and value.

Getting Paid

Now it's time to get paid. How much do you charge for your inventory on your podcast? It's quite simple! How much is it worth? Are you building a podcast for the first time and don't have content yet recorded? Or, do you have a ton of content recorded and need help monetising it?

Well, if you're just starting out, let's be honest it's going to be a challenge to get the first sponsors spots sold. Once you land one, then go after another, then another. Sell them for whatever you can get for them but I recommend you set your structure like this.

Commercials spots are $499 for 10 episodes for 12 months. What this means is, their 30-second commercial will air for 12-months on 10 episodes of your podcast. Remember I told you to build a 10-episode series. This is why. So the numbers are easy to navigate and understand for the client. Give them those episodes for a year. Meaning if they don't want to renew in a year's time, you can now sell that inventory all over again to another client but don't have to record another episode of your show. Remember, you're building this into a system.

I currently have about 500 hours of podcasts recorded and for the most part only record commercials these days which means that after only five years in business I am only working a few hours a day and living the life I have always dreamed of.

Sell your interviews for $199. What's nice is, you can always give your client a deal if they want an interview and commercials, drop the price by $100 and make the deal happen. Nobody said you have to price gouge people. If you take care of them, they are most likely going to send you referrals. It's crazy how easy this works.

So, let's talk revenue. How much money are we talking about here? Let's break it down by a 10-episode series.

If you have 6 sponsors per show and you're charging $499 per 30-seconds, you're netting $2994.00 for 10 episodes. Let's talk commercials now.

If you have 9 commercials per show and you're charging $499 per 30-seconds, you're grossing another $4491.00 for 10 episodes. Now you're at $7485.00 in 10 weeks time. Now let's look at revenue from guests.

If you have 4 guests per episode and you're charging $199 per guest spot, that's $796.00 per episode. Multiply by 10 episodes in a series and you're at $7960.00. Now add this to the advertising revenue and you're at $15,445.00 in just 10 weeks.

How does this model shake out in a year's time? You will gross $80,314 over 12 months. Once you have built one and get the hang of it, build a second show, then a third, then a fourth and so on. Like I said before, I currently have 21 shows. If you had only 10 shows and were selling inventory in all of those shows, you're looking at $803,140 annually. Now let's talk about building commercials.

Building Commercials

Building commercials are easy. I mean, they are really easy. Just remember, who what why where how? Always provide a solution to a problem and don't over complicate it.

For this book, I would say something like, "For over 20 years, Jon Robert Quinn has been helping small businesses reach a larger audience and increase sales. If you're struggling to make ends meet or just want to increase production, visit JRQTV.com today, again JRQTV.com."

It's literally that simple. Imagine people sending you $499 and you sit in front of a microphone for literally 2 minutes recording a commercial and then maybe another 2 minutes to edit and about 10 minutes to insert into the show structure and then upload to the server to distribute the RSS to the outlets like Spotify, TuneIn, etc. I'm not speaking lies here. This is literally what I do all day long. I also write books and help with other marketing too such as billboards, apps and websites. But for the most part, this is the extent of my business. You ready?

Structuring Shows

Structuring Shows is equally as easy as commercials. Picture this… You have your interviews already recorded. Your commercials are also recorded. So now you just need to set your "block" time. So your commercial block consists of 3 commercials correct? Save as "block 1" for commercial break 1. Do the same with "block 2" and "block 3" for commercials breaks 2 and 3.

Create a block for your opener and closer, then all you need to do to structure shows is insert your interviews and save into appropriate folders to stay organised.

When you save the file, use "Jon Robert Quinn Interview - R1". When you sell new commercials or need to insert new commercials, save the file as "Jon Robert Quinn Interview - R2". The content stays the same in terms of interviews. The only difference are the commercials. This allows the audience to stay familiar with the show and who's on those shows. The only thing changing are the ads in the show.

Over the course over 2 or 3 years, you'll be growing the audience of those episodes but periodically be changing the ads inserted into the shows because that is sponsor inventory and that inventory is very valuable. As time go one, you will find yourself selling the ads for more money in R5 or R6 shows than you did in R1 and R2 shows. This is because you have increased your value and still getting paid from work you did years ago. It's a wonderful feeling.

Distribution

This is a very exciting time. You're now ready to get your product out to the masses. The simplest and most efficient way to do this is to upload onto SoundCloud. Use their Pro package and spend the $20 per month or whatever it costs. It's worth every penny. I used to pay $2400 per month on radio with no analytics and today I pay a fraction and can provide my clients with listener numbers. That's huge!!!

Upload your file "Jon Robert Quinn - R1" to SoundCloud. Remember we titled your show after whoever your guest was. Just make sure that you're using the R1, R2, R3 in your title. This is simply a guide to know what ads are running.

What's really nice about SoundCloud Pro is that you can REPLACE files and update the title. What this means is, once you replace ads in a show, you can then replace the R1 file with R2 on SoundCloud and change the title to read R2 and it WILL NOT affect your play count or analytics. This prevents you from having to delete episodes and start the counter at 1. You will keep your play count by replacing the existing file. This is HUGE!!!

Now let's talk distribution. The RSS feed SoundCloud creates for you is GOLD. By visiting Apple Podcast Submitter, Spotify, TuneIn, Luminary and a variety of other sources, all they need is the RSS feed from SoundCloud and the rest is magic. The feed sends your files everywhere and the play counts from those streaming services reflect your

SoundCloud play numbers giving you the analytics you need to provide more value to your clients. Is all of this making sense yet? Let's talk branding.

Building Your Empire

With any business, branding is very important.

This is where your empire is built. From here, you start creating T-shirts and sell from your site attached to your Podcast. Create an App that makes accessing your content even easier.

Do you have a logo or something that makes your brand stand out? Your social media, App, Podcast, Shirts and Merch should all have your brand attached. Start appearing on other shows and charge to be on their show. Start charging to speak to groups of people and teach your specialty to other people that need the knowledge.

Get on Instagram and give little one-minute clips of your shows to your audience with appropriate hashtags to drive traffic to your podcast. It's really not hard to become an internet sensation. All it takes is a little bit of work.

No excuses, now get out there and make it happen.

www.ingramcontent.com/pod-product-compliance
Lightning Source LLC
Chambersburg PA
CBHW021503210526
45463CB00002B/864